curious about

MEMORIAL DAY

BY AMY HOUTS

AMICUS LEARNING

What are you

CHAPTER ONE

An Important Holiday
PAGE **4**

CHAPTER TWO

The History of Memorial Day
PAGE **10**

curious about?

CHAPTER THREE

Let's Celebrate!
PAGE **16**

Stay Curious! Learn More 22
Glossary. 24
Index 24

Curious About is published by
Amicus Learning, an imprint of Amicus
P.O. Box 227, Mankato, MN 56002
www.amicuspublishing.us

Copyright © 2026 Amicus.
International copyright reserved in all countries.
No part of this book may be reproduced in any
form without written permission from the publisher.

Editor: Ana Brauer
Series Designer: Kathleen Petelinsek
Book Designer and Photo Researcher: Sara Hood

Library of Congress Cataloging-in-Publication Data
Names: Houts, Amy, 1957- author
Title: Curious about Memorial Day / Amy Houts.
Description: Mankato, MN : Amicus Learning, 2026. |
Series: Curious about holidays | Includes bibliographical
references and index. | Audience: Ages 6–9 | Audience:
Grades 2–3 | Summary: "Discover the importance of Memorial
Day! Learn about Memorial Day's history, significance,
and celebrations in this question-and-answer book for
elementary-aged readers. Includes table of contents, glossary,
further resources, and index"—Provided by publisher.
Identifiers: LCCN 2025014056 (print) | LCCN 2025014057
(ebook) | ISBN 9798892008495 library binding | ISBN
9798892009157 paperback | ISBN 9798892009812 ebook
Subjects: LCSH: Memorial Day—Juvenile literature
Classification: LCC E642 .H85 2026 (print) | LCC E642
(ebook) | DDC 394.261—dc23/eng/20250509
LC record available at https://lccn.loc.gov/2025014056
LC ebook record available at https://lccn.loc.gov/2025014057

Photo Credits: Alamy Stock Photo/B Christopher, 9 (top); US
Army Photo, 15, US Navy Photo, 3, 17 (middle), Walter Bibikow,
5; Getty Images/ALEX WROBLEWSKI, 16, rhyman007, 2, 12,
kali9, 6–7, Martin Ruegner, 20–21, Michelle Mengsu Chang/
Toronto Star, 18, Paul Morigi, 17 (bottom), Peter Unger, 10–11,
Spencer Platt, 17 (top); VCG, 19, WHL, 17 (second from top);
Zhu Ziyu/VCG, 17 (second from top); Shutterstock/KAZMAT, 14,
Michael Shake, 2, 9 (bottom), Sergii Figurnyi, cover, 1; The Noun
Project/Lulah, 22, 23, P Thanga Vignesh, 22, 23; Wikimedia
Commons/Thure de Thulstrup, 8

Every effort has been made to contact copyright holders for
material reproduced in this book. Any omissions will be rectified
in subsequent printings if notice is given to the publisher.

Printed in United States of America

CHAPTER ONE

What is Memorial Day?

Memorial Day is a day to remember **veterans** who died. Veterans are soldiers, sailors, and **airmen**. They fought for our **freedom**. Veterans include all people who have served in the United States armed forces.

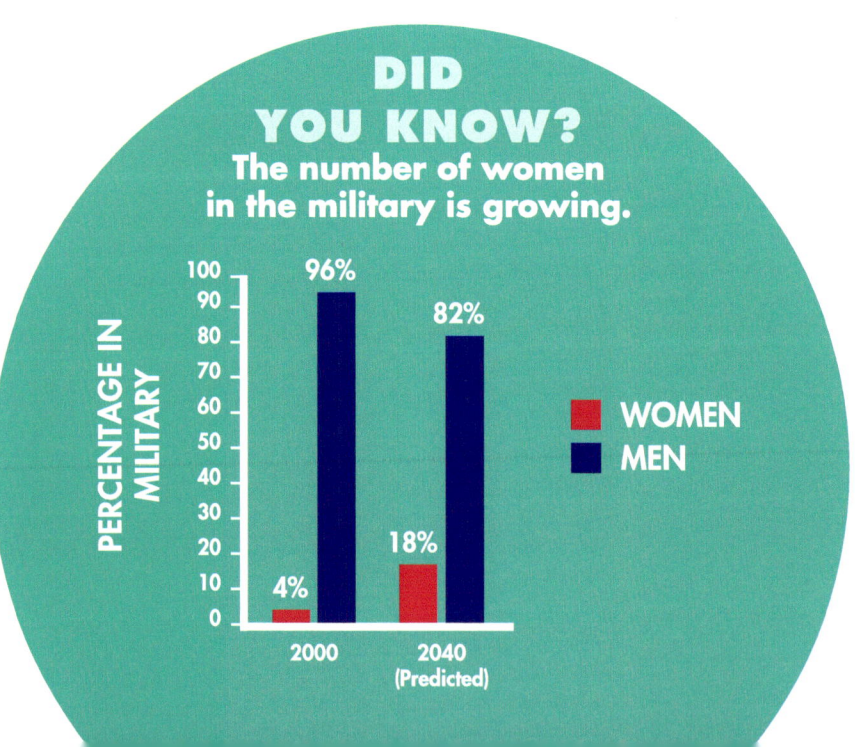

DID YOU KNOW?
The number of women in the military is growing.

AN IMPORTANT HOLIDAY

Memorial Day honors veterans across the United States.

AN IMPORTANT HOLIDAY

AN IMPORTANT HOLIDAY

Who celebrates Memorial Day?

6

Many people get the day off school or work for Memorial Day.

AN IMPORTANT HOLIDAY

People in the United States. It's an American holiday. People who are veterans celebrate. But you don't need to be a veteran. Anyone in the United States can celebrate Memorial Day.

AN IMPORTANT HOLIDAY

The Civil War was fought from 1861 to 1865.

Why is Memorial Day important?

It is a day to say thank you to the veterans who died. Memorial Day started after the Civil War. Now people honor those who died in other wars. That includes wars before and after the Civil War.

The Vietnam Memorial in Washington, D.C., lists the names of the soldiers who died in the Vietnam War.

The WWII Memorial honors the bravery of people who fought long ago.

AN IMPORTANT HOLIDAY

CHAPTER TWO 2

How long has Memorial Day been celebrated?

People started celebrating in 1866. The Civil War was over. Many soldiers and sailors had died. People **decorated** their graves with flowers. But Memorial Day had a different name. It was called Decoration Day. The name changed over time.

Many veterans are buried at Arlington National **Cemetery** in Virginia.

THE HISTORY OF MEMORIAL DAY

Leaving flowers is a way to say thank you to veterans.

When do people celebrate Memorial Day?

Decoration Day was first celebrated on May 30, 1868. People would leave poppies and other flowers at gravesites. Flowers grow in May. This is why the holiday is in May. Some people still celebrate on May 30. But now the national holiday is the last Monday in May.

On Memorial Day, flags fly halfway down to remember soldiers.

What do people do for Memorial Day?

People fly the American flag at **half-staff**. This is a sign of mourning and respect to those who died. People also pick or buy flowers. They visit a cemetery to place flowers on the graves of veterans. They place American flags, too.

DID YOU KNOW? At 3 p.m. local time, many Americans have a moment of silence to honor fallen soldiers.

A soldier leaves American flags at the graves of veterans.

CHAPTER THREE
3

How do people celebrate Memorial Day?

Many towns hold a Memorial Day parade.

People get together with family. They attend memorial services. They watch parades. The biggest parade is the National Memorial Day Parade. It takes place in Washington, D.C. The National Memorial Day Concert is held there, too.

PARADES

MEMORIAL SERVICES

FLAG RAISING

VISITING GRAVESITES

CONCERTS

MEMORIAL DAY CELEBRATIONS

17

LET'S CELEBRATE!

Kids help place flags in Canada to honor veterans for Remembrance Day.

How do other countries honor their veterans?

In Russia, people honor veterans with music and parades.

LET'S CELEBRATE!

Canada's holiday is called Remembrance Day. It's held on November 11. That's the day when World War I ended. Russia's holiday is called Victory Day. It's held May 9. That's the day they defeated Nazi Germany in World War II.

What's the difference between Memorial Day and Veterans Day?

LET'S CELEBRATE!

Americans celebrate November 11, too. It is called Veterans Day. Veterans Day is like Memorial Day. Both holidays celebrate our veterans. But Memorial Day is for veterans who died. Veterans Day honors all veterans. It celebrates those who died and those who are alive.

STAY CURIOUS!

ASK MORE QUESTIONS

What are some symbols of Memorial Day?

What does the US president do to celebrate Memorial Day?

Try a BIG QUESTION: How is Memorial Day celebrated where I live?

SEARCH FOR ANSWERS

Search the library catalog or the Internet.
A librarian, teacher, or parent can help you.

Using Keywords
Find the looking glass.

Keywords are the most important words in your question.

If you want to know about:
- symbols of Memorial Day, type: MEMORIAL DAY SYMBOLS
- how the president spends Memorial Day, type: PRESIDENT MEMORIAL DAY

LEARN MORE

FIND GOOD SOURCES

Here are some good, safe sources you can use in your research.
Your librarian can help you find more.

Books

A Day for Rememberin'
by Leah Henderson and Floyd Cooper, 2021.

Twenty-One Steps
by Jeff Gottesfeld and Matt Tavares, 2021.

Internet Sites

Britannica Kids | Memorial Day
https://kids.britannica.com/kids/article/Memorial-Day/399542
This site provides information about Memorial Day and its history.

U.S. Department of Veteran Affairs | Memorial Day
https://www.cem.va.gov/history/Memorial-Day-history.asp#
This site provides information about Memorial Day history.

Every effort has been made to ensure that these websites are appropriate for children. However, because of the nature of the Internet, it's impossible to guarantee that these sites will remain active indefinitely or that their contents will not be altered.

SHARE AND TAKE ACTION

Be quiet for one minute at 3 p.m. on Memorial Day.
Be thankful for the men and women who served our country.

Fly the American flag.
Ask a parent to help you fly an American flag half-staff on Memorial Day.

Visit a cemetery. Ask a parent to take you to a cemetery on Memorial Day.
Bring flowers to place on veterans' graves.

GLOSSARY

airman A person who serves in the air force or navy.

cemetery A place where dead people are buried.

decorate To make more attractive by adding something that is beautiful or becoming.

freedom Being able to act and speak in the way you want.

half-staff Flying a flag halfway down the flagpole.

veteran A former member of the armed forces especially during wartime.

INDEX

Civil War, 8, 11
concerts, 16, 17
Decoration Day, 11, 13
flowers, 11, 12, 13, 14
half-staff, 14
parades, 16, 17, 19
Remembrance Day (Canada), 18, 19
Veterans Day, 20–21
Victory Day (Russia), 19
World War I, 19
World War II, 9, 19

About the Author

Amy Houts is the author of more than 100 picture books, and she loves writing about holidays. She celebrates Memorial Day by visiting a cemetery in Iowa to honor her husband's family. When she is not writing, you can find her walking her dog in Northwest Missouri.